Please Talk to Me, God!

Donald L. Deffner

Publishing House
St. Louis

Photo credits: Diane Spiess Young, p.p. 17, 25. Walter Chandoha, p. 33. Lief Ericksenn, p.p. 52, 61. David S. Strickler, p. 80.

Copyright © 1983 Concordia Publishing House
3558 S. Jefferson Avenue, St. Louis, MO 63118
Manufactured in the United States of America

Library of Congress Cataloging in Publication Data

Deffner, Donald L.
    Please talk to me, God!

    1. Christian life—Lutheran authors. I. Title.
BV4501.2.D428 1983   248.4'841   82-25271
ISBN 0-570-03899-5 (pbk.)

1 2 3 4 5 6 7 8 9 10 CB 92 91 90 89 88 87 86 85 84 83

Preface

The Lord is with you when you are with Him. And if you seek Him, He will let you find Him.
2 Chronicles 15:2 NASB

For some people God is just not a present, pulsating Reality in their lives. How tragic when He *has* revealed Himself to us in Jesus Christ, Who goes striding through the Gospels as a very real flesh and blood person.

God wants us to know Him through His Son. He wants us to listen to Him in His Word and to be empowered by Him through the Sacraments.

He is really quite a discoverable and contemporary God. And I submit that if we do not know Him personally, one of the reasons is that we don't intentionally trust and act on His promises—of which there are nearly 9,000 in the Scriptures.

In two earlier volumes, *You Promised Me, God!* and *Come Closer to Me, God!* (Concordia) I have sought to depict the loving nature of God as I have come to know Him in the Old and New Testaments. There I dealt with His promises and challenges throughout the Scriptures. In this volume I further explore His call to move out more into our community and the world—still assured by His powerful pledge that He is always with us.

Where a number (1) appears with a vignette it corresponds to the author listed at the end who is to be credited for the statement(s) or germinal idea behind the piece.

May the Holy Spirit bless your meditations on these promises and loving challenges from our Lord, that you may grow stronger in reliance on the One who made them—the Promiser Himself.

How This Book Can Be Used

Each of us finds that God fulfills His promises to us in different ways. But we can still share that experience with others and encourage those needing help to search the Scriptures and hear the voice of a loving Father talking to His beloved children.

This could be done in small groups where a vignette is read, after which the Scripture passages are examined in a variety of translations. Then individuals might share ways in which a particular promise or challenge of God has been evidenced in his or her life.

And then—why not write some yourself?

Contents

THE CHRISTIAN ASKS—
How can I live better
with myself, God?
GOD RESPONDS—

Seven Miles to Sin

A church
down there
claimed it was
"seven miles
from any known
form of sin"
How foolish!
Evil is
within you
Search your heart
and see
But also look
and you will see
the "Christ-within-you"
He is
the Chief Character
in your life
and the Power
to overcome both
the evil within
and the evil without[1]

Mark 7:21-23   Colossians 1:27

Unlocking Your Creativity

You may not be
a genius
But you do have
a chance
A chance to unlock
the powers within you
which I have given you
You have a chance
So take My dare
Examine your gifts
such as they are
Study
Work
Risk
Ask My guidance
Live in hope
Remember the man
in prison many years
who one day
tried the door
and found it
unlocked

2 Timothy 1:6   *1 Corinthians 12:1-11*

Real Fulfillment

It's not just in
getting to know
the real inner "you"
or in stretching your mind
to find wisdom
that one finds fulfillment
So don't escape from the world

that needs your service
and actualized love
but lay down
your life
for it
as did
My Son
That's the deepest love
of all
He
doing My will
suffered and died
for you
Now learn
from
Him

1 Corinthians 1:17-21   1 Peter 2:21

The "Others"

You say you
are appalled
at the callousness
and indifference
of others
to the needs and hurts
of people
And you say
you are amazed
at the incredible lengths
to which My love goes
in encompassing them
and their selfish lives
Yes
My love

is beyond fathoming
But
did you ever think
of yourself
as one
of those
"others"?

Deuteronomy 15:17

Surrender

Often behind
your inner turmoil
is your unrelenting criticism
of yourself
But learn from My Word
how I love you
as you are
not as you
ought to be
While you sinned
I still loved you
(though what you did
grieved Me)
So surrender your heart
and not just your mind
to this truth
My Son died for you
You are forgiven
Accepted
Loved
Now don't be
so judgmental
toward yourself

Romans 5:8   Joel 2:13   Psalm 130:4

Are You Rigid?

Are you rigid?
inflexible?
unbending?
Do you live
by law
or by love?
I've given you commandments
so you won't hurt yourself
or others
But I did it
out of love
not to hamper you
Live in love then
Not rigidly
but relaxedly
Observe My commandments
But at the same time
enjoy
the freedom I gave you

Romans 6:14   Romans 8:15-17

The Real Dictator

The dictator
who would tyrannize you
and rob you
of your freedom
which you have
in My Son
is not
an external power
but a force
within *you*

Recognize it
Let My Son's
indwelling Spirit
subdue it
overcome it
replace it
Then you will be
truly free

Mark 7:21-23   Luke 6:45   Romans 2:5
Colossians 1:27   John 8:36

You Know

You know
and
I know
there are many ways
of killing yourself
besides
obvious suicide
overindulgence
in many forms
Eating too much
Driving too fast
Drinking too much
Working too hard
I care for you
Take care
of yourself
You know
and
I
know
Why

Philippians 3:17-19   Philippians 4:5

The Proper Criteria

I do not
want you to be
a master in competition
a "success"
as the world
measures values
If you must compete
compete with yourself
Ask rather
"Am I using my God-given gifts
to the utmost
of my ability?"
"Am I *faithful?*"
Those are
My criteria
of values

2 Timothy 1:6   1 Corinthians 4:2

You Are Unique

Be the unique person
I made you to be
Accept the
stamp of personality
I gave you
There is no one
in all my
creation
just like you
So resist the
cult of conformity
around you
Persist against

peer pressure
Be My individual
and not just
one of the bland
being led
by the bland[2]

Isaiah 49:16   *Romans 12:1-2*

Three Basic Needs

I know
you need
Acceptance
Affection
Achievement
But those
don't involve
what others
think of you
but what you
think of yourself
Not too highly
Apostle Paul advises
At the same time
I think very highly
of you
Enough
to give you
My Son

Romans 12:3   *Romans 8:32*

Robber Ghosts

Do you
want freedom
from the robber ghosts
which plague
your inner being?
Try to get free
from that which
restrains you
and you will feel
your bondage to
those evil habits
which enslave you
If you will
let My Son
dwell in you
you will know
what real freedom is
Do you really
want to be
free?

1 John 4:16   2 Corinthians 5:17   John 8:36

Your Real Self

"Know yourself"
said the ancient philosopher
True
up to a point
But *ultimate* reality
means not only seeking
to know yourself
but Christ Jesus
My Son

For your identity
is to be
with Him
and only when
you know Him
will you really know
the "self"
I want you
to be

Galatians 2:20   *1 John 4:16-17*

Prayer

Lord, please help me to recognize the true nature of my inner being which is so often self-centered. Forgive me! Mold me! Renew me! Make me daily your new creation that I may become the self-in-Christ You want me to be. In the strong name of Jesus Christ. Amen.

THE CHRISTIAN ASKS—
How can I relate better
to my partner, God?
GOD RESPONDS—

Creativity Insecurity

When you
And your partner
fail each other
hurt each other
really want to
destroy the other
let that be
the precise moment
for *creative insecurity*
At that point
intentionally realize
you are both
forgiven sinners
in My eyes
So forgive each other
even though
you don't agree
For then
through My Spirit
I will give you
a new start
and the divine miracle
of a fresh relationship
will begin[3]

*Mark 11:25   Luke 17:4   Ephesians 4:32
Colossians 3:13   John 15:5*

Saying or Doing?

I affirm
your value
your development
your creativity
your potential
Do you
do the same
of your partner?
In My Son
I gave Myself
totally
for you
Do you give
unstintingly
unselfishly
without reward
for the person
you *say*
you love?

John 15:12   Ephesians 5:2
Colossians 3:14

From Pillar to Post

When will you
stop moving
from pillar to post
restlessly
looking for
the person who
will please *you*
rather than
struggling with

the inner "you"
who pleases neither
Me
you
nor your partner?
Contend rather with
the potential you
the "Christ in you"
By the Holy Spirit's power
learn how to be
free to give
and free to affirm
your partner
as well as
you affirm
your Christ-self
For right now
I
affirm
you[4]

Colossians 1:27   *Matthew 20:28*
Galatians 2:20

A House of Strangers

You idealized
that new relationship
with your partner
A fantasy-filled
perfect "us"
And later then
you saw
you had been
only strangers
And you had neither given
nor taken

but merely
made use
of each other
each for
your own purpose
How horrible!
Can you only love
an image
of your own imagination?
Are you ultimately
unloving
and unlovable?
No!
Learn from My Son
Pour yourself out
Empty
deny yourself
My Holy Spirit
will give you
the power
and you will learn
what *real* love
is[5]

James 5:16   Ephesians 4:17-27
Ephesians 5:22-33   Philippians 2:5-15

The Right Source

Do not try
to solve that problem
with your partner
with some power
you feel is latent
within you
For you

will fail
But I your Father
can give you
a power
and a peace
that passes
all understanding
It is limitless
free
and you may
borrow all
you wish
from Me

Psalm 121:2   Philippians 4:17

Not Worth Understanding

A man was upset
because his wife
intimated that she
saw through him
better than he did
And she was infuriated
because he assumed
she wasn't worth
the trouble of
understanding
How tragic!
My children
My children!
If you are
faithful to Me
then you can be
free!
Not just to *use*

but capable to love
and able to affirm
your partner's value
and development
as much as
your own
But separated from Me
your "freedom"
is a bondage
You are
self-enslaved
Your "love"
a mere
exploitation
But *in* Me
you are
"free to love"
I mean
really
love![4] [5]

Matthew 7:5   *Philippians 2:4*
1 Corinthians 10:33   *2 Corinthians 8:9*
John 8:36

Prayer

Lord, please be merciful and forgive me for the times I have hurt my partner. By Your Holy Spirit enable both of us to forgive each other and to live selflessly for each other. And create a fresh bond of peace and mutual helpfulness between us that we may, by Your Holy Spirit's power, do Your will—both where we live now, and wherever you call us to serve. In the strong name of Jesus Christ. Amen.

THE CHRISTIAN ASKS—
How can I be more faithful, God?
GOD RESPONDS—

The Why of Going

Spirituality
is not a trait
but
self-denying
sacrificial giving
Prayer is not
certain words
but a *life*
of justice
and mercy
given over
to others
The true church
doesn't just "go"
but remembers *why*
The church goes
to reflect
Me who established it
The God of
liberation
and
committed love

Ephesians 5:2

Love Love Love

As you know
there are so many
different kinds
of love
What do you love?
Your partner?
Your car?
Your pet?
Your favorite team?
Your work?
Your hobby?
I affirm
all those
They are My presents
to you
But I have
only one question
Do you *really*
love
Me?

Deuteronomy 10:12   Psalm 31:23
Jude 21

The Right Questions

Do you just
come
see
and concur
when you go
to a church meeting?
Or do you
(without undue skepticism)

challenge
probe
question
as to whether
it is *My* work
which is really
going on?
Whether your purpose
is *My* purpose?
And whether it is
the Gospel
(or something else)
on which you are
relying
to do
the job?

Acts 5:34-39   1 Corinthians 10:31

Your First Thought

Be honest
with Me
now
What do you
cherish
the most?
What really
turns you on?
What is
the first thing
you think about
when you awaken
in the morning?
(I hope
you're thinking

of Me)
Remember
As you think
in your heart
so
you
are

Matthew 6:19-21   Mark 12:30

That's What Fathers Are For

I hear you
asking Me for things
quite often
I like that
That's what fathers are for
And I've answered
all of your requests
(in My own way)
But how recently
have you thanked Me
for My answers
to your prayers?

Matthew 6:9   Ephesians 5:20

The Goal of Life

Standing up
for My truth
is the greatest thing
you can do
in the world
The goal

of your life
is not
happiness
It is not
achieving pleasure
and
avoiding pain
Rather it is
doing My will
come
what
may

Matthew 7:21   Revelation 22:14
Matthew 12:50   John 14:23

Actuality

Not doctrine divorced
from life
Not just intellectual theory
but practice
Not only creed
but deed
Not just
going to church
but being
the church
Not just words
but actions
Not just
mystical emotion
but sacrifice
Not just prayers
but bread
for the hungry

Not just weeping for
but being crushed
for a
broken world
like
My
Son

James 1:25   *1 John 3:18*

Your Plans or Mine?

I see you had
some big plans
for Me
Or rather it was
your *own* idea
of My plans
for you
Hold on
Which do you want?
Your plans
or Mine?
Let go
and let Me
take over
For I have plans
you have no idea about
Which do you
really want?
Your plans?
Or Mine?

Jeremiah 29:11-13

Prayer

Lord, by the power of Your Holy Spirit give me the grace each day to be faithful to You. To trust You fully even though the way ahead is not clear to me. To rest confidently in the assurance of Your abiding love, leaning on Your sure promises, but even more, on You, the *Promiser*. In the strong name of Jesus Christ. Amen.

THE CHRISTIAN SAYS—
I need forgiveness, God!
GOD RESPONDS—

No "Iffy" Forgiveness

Do not think
if you believe
then I will act
and forgive you
My love is
not conditional
or achievable
It is a gift
and not *dependent*
on your believing
So
never forget
My forgiveness
is
already
there

Romans 5:8   *2 Corinthians 9:15*
James 1:17

Guilt

If your past life
was totally open
to public view
every thought known
every word heard
every deed revealed

then you
would do more
than blush
And yet
you need not
live in guilt
No need
to fear
My grace
is near

Hebrews 4:12-13, 16

Two Different "Gifts"

You gave My Son
that
which sent Him
to the cross
He gave you
that
which brings you
to heaven

Romans 6:23

A Cheery Discovery

You can't earn
My forgiveness
offered you
through My Son
You can't merit it
achieve it
deserve it
But you can

accept it
enjoy it
be thankful for it
Freely then receive
My righteousness
as a cover
for your sin
That was Luther's
cheery discovery
Make it
yours

Ephesians 2:8-9   Hebrews 4:16
Psalm 31   Romans 5

Prayer

Lord, keep me ever mindful of the high cost of forgiveness—the death of Your Son, my Savior. But assure me also—each day—that this forgiveness is mine when I come to You in penitent faith, trusting in Your mercy. And set me free from the plaguing memory of guilt over past sin, knowing Your blessed promise that when You forgive, You forget. In the strong name of Jesus Christ. Amen.

THE CHRISTIAN ASKS—
How can I handle despair, God?
GOD RESPONDS—

Depressed? Sing!

When you are depressed
sing hymns and psalms
(Even if
you can't carry a tune
hum it in your head)
Give thanks to Me
For then you are
dealing with
Ultimate Reality
I know it is
hard to do
But I will give you
the power
For
I am your Father
I will bend evil
in your life
and bring it
to good
for you
That's
a promise!

Psalm 147:7   Isaiah 51:3   Acts 16:25
Ephesians 5:19-20   James 5:13

Learning How to Cast

The secret
of overcoming anxiety
is not in
forgetting it
repressing it
ignoring it
suppressing it
But like
a good fisherman
casting it
into My lap
I will handle it
Focus on Me
Praise Me
Praise Me
Praise Me
That's the first step
in coping with
anxiety

1 Peter 5:6-11   Psalms 145—150

Really Need a Psychiatrist?

You *may*
But then again
you may *not*
need a psychiatrist
You may not
be manic-depressive
psychotic
You *may* not suffer
from a trauma
a repression

or a fixation
But you may need
more worship
of Me
more reading
of your Bible
more meaningful prayer
and more giving
of yourself
to others around you
You *may*
need a psychiatrist
and then again
you may not

1 Thessalonians 3:12   Hebrews 6:1   1 Peter 2:2
2 Peter 1:5-6   2 Peter 3:18

A Lot of Trust

Remember this
Though I know
you do not want
the illness
or tragedy
or trial
which presently
afflicts you
Nevertheless
be assured
that I trust you
a great deal
in permitting it
to happen
to you

Hebrews 12:1-13

The Rock

You must learn
to live
with the insecurities
uncertainties
and ambiguities
of life
But know this
I am secure
I am certain
I am not ambiguous
In the storm
I am your Rock
that cannot
be moved
I
am your
God

Deuteronomy 32:15   2 Samuel 22:2-7
Psalm 31:2   1 Corinthians 10:4

Prayer

Lord, teach me each day not to wallow in my despair but to cast my care upon You. Direct my attention away from my worries to focus upon You and Your infinite love for me. Also lead me to and through the rich resources of Your Word that I would see the way You would have me go. Guide me! Move me! Bear me up, O Lord! In the strong of Jesus Christ. Amen.

THE CHRISTIAN ASKS—
How do You feel about me, God?
GOD RESPONDS—

True Confession

A woman
down there
confessed fornication
seduction and
impatience with her children
But her pastor
would not absolve her
until she admitted
the real reason
she had done
those things
was to spite Me
and the Church
That penitent confession
being made
absolution was announced
And when the woman
said it was so good
to be back with the church
the pastor said
"We never
let you go"
You know what?
I never had
either[6]

1 John 1:4-9   Hebrews 13:5b

Maybe You Won't

Maybe you won't
get well
keep your job
see your child
free of problems
Maybe you won't
reach that goal
keep that treasure
find that fulfillment
But My love
will be shown you
sustaining your spirit
changing *apparent* evil
into good
and blessing
when you lean
on Me
and
My promises

Genesis 50:20   *Hebrews 13:5b*
Psalm 37:28

On Being in Love

You know
I like
just being
with you
around you
near you
I love you
Your sheer presence
is My joy

and My happiness
I made you
as a unique person
in My kingdom
My Son
died for you
Now there
is love!
Now you may not
need to die
to prove your love
for Me
But do you
like being
near Me
"in love"
as I like
being close
to you?

John 21:15-17   1 John 4:19

Real Value

You are not
deserving
of My love
But you are worth
much
to Me
You are not
good enough to Me
but then
you
can never be
My Son

took care
of it all
His death
and resurrection
redeemed you
Now
that's
value!

Titus 3:5   Romans 5   Romans 8

Just the Right Size

Do not be
so proud
of your
humility
(Maybe you
have much
to be humble
about)
And yet
in *My* eyes
I
I
your loving Father
say that
you
you
are important
Important enough
to
die
for

Romans 12:3   John 3:16
Romans 5:8   1 John 3:1

I Challenge You

I want you to grow
use your gifts
accept your limitations
control your appetites
live in moderation
and yet
be yourself
My child
unique
as I have
created you
Quite a challenge
isn't it!
Enjoy!

Philippians 4:4-7

The Search

"I'm searching
for God"
said the woman
That's not how it is
For I had been looking
for her
for a long time
She was lost
I never
have been
My Son
the Good Shepherd
risked
and then gave
His life

reaching over a precipice
for that one
lost sheep
Let's get it straight
You're not really looking
for Me
as much as
I
am looking
for you

2 Chronicles 15:2   *John 10:14-15*

Prayer

Lord, through Your Holy Spirit and Your Blessed Word help me to see again and again Your searching for me, Your limitless love for me, Your patience with me, Your desire for me to be ever near You, Your forgiving me, Your freeing me, Your affirming me!— and all through the life, death, resurrection and ascension of Your beloved Son. In the strong name of Jesus Christ. Amen.

THE CHRISTIAN ASKS—
How can I serve You better, God?
GOD RESPONDS—

My Ambassador

Christianity should be
a comfort
to a distressed mind
True
But not to avoid
reality
and responsibility
Rather it should
strengthen
confront
identify who you are
in My eyes
and then
motivate you to be
My agent
of hope
to serve the world
Are you willing
to be
My ambassador?

Isaiah 61:1-3   Ephesians 6:20
1 Thessalonians 5:11

The Mailbox

Over the years
I've written you
many love-letters
through My prophets
and the apostles
and my other
secretaries
Did you enjoy
the treat
at the mailbox?
Who needs
a love-letter
from you
today?

1 John 1:4   2 Peter 3:1-2

The Blessing of Fulfilling Work

Remember to
give Me
genuine thanks
each day
for the privilege
and blessing
of fulfilling work
For it can be
your "salvation"
Idleness
boredom
and noninvolvement
create a workshop
for

The Enemy Below
Remember
he has plenty
for you
to do
So thank Me
daily
for the
privilege
and *blessing*
of fulfilling
work

John 9:4   1 Timothy 2:8

 ## Give It Away!

Only in giving
of yourself
for Me
and My children
around you
is space created
within you
that you
may receive more
For then you
are able to
give still more
of yourself
And again be
refilled
indeed
fulfilled!

Matthew 10:8   Luke 6:30-38
2 Corinthians 9:7

6-8

58

No Deal!

It's not
a "deal"
but a question
For no one
can bargain
with Me
And you
can never
pay Me back
But I
have a question
I gave
My Son
for you
What have
you
given
to
Me?

Ephesians 2:8-9   *1 Peter 2:5-9*
Hebrews 13:15-16

Your Present Life-Style

All those things
you've been
throwing yourself
into lately
Sublimations
of all kinds
What do your
friends outside the church
think about your religion?

Do they sense
that you aren't
really satisfied and
that you are not really
that different
from them?
In terms of
your present life-style
are they starting
to get the message
that
I
don't
really
satisfy?

Ephesians 5:1-20   1 Peter 2:11-12

The Tyranny of Freedom

So you want
to be
absolutely free?
Can you handle
the "tyranny" of freedom?
For with real freedom
comes real responsibility
Do you
really want
freedom *from* something
or freedom *for* something?
Give Me your self
Be My loving servant
Surrender to Me
And discover
(to your joy!)

that in total acquiescence
you will find
total freedom
And I will
give you back
a new "I"

2 Corinthians 5:17   *John 8:36*

 Acceptance

I have accepted
you
even though
you have done
quite a few
unacceptable things
Acceptance is essential
In fact I have
accepted you *totally*
through the death
and resurrection
of My Son Jesus
Now will you
accept the "unacceptable"?
love the "unlovable"?
desire to help
the "undesirable" ones
who are very near
to you
Just look for them
They are not
very far
away

Romans 5:8   John 15:9-14

Four Little Words

Not just when
special gifts
come your way
But as you eat
as you drink
as you drive
as you enjoy
the treasure of life
the privilege of work
the joy of leisure
the fervor of love
the sound of music
So savor it now and
with four little words
sent in My
direction
"This is a blessing"
Say it
now

1 Corinthians 10:31

Prayer

Lord, teach me to pray for open doors to help my neighbor. But then move me, Lord, to actually walk through those doors (the "servants' entrance") to be Your ambassador to a suffering and sorrowing world. And may I go in the spirit and the name of Your Son, who came not to be ministered unto, but to minister. In the strong name of Jesus Christ. Amen.

THE CHRISTIAN ASKS—
How can I learn more about You, God?
GOD RESPONDS—

Deep Sea Diving

As you approach
My Holy Scriptures
don't just read them
but meditate
and "pray" them
For Scripture resists
casual perusal
but yields the
fruits of wisdom
to the earnest searcher
So come penitently
and learn to be
a sounder
of the depths
a diver
a researcher
and then
you will be
a receiver of
great treasure
My Holy Spirit

Psalm 119:97-105   Ezekiel 36:27
John 8:31-32   Acts 1:8

Proper Prayer

When you pray
do so in the name
of My Son Jesus
Pray in faith
not wavering
and My Spirit
will aid you
Focus on Me
and My will
for you
As you pray
identify with the pain
and brokenness of your neighbor
Offer it up to Me
And do not dwell on yourself
or on a fantasy
about what you need
but rather on
what you really believe
I will know what
will be best for you
And I promise
I will hear
and I will answer

Romans 8:26   James 1:6   Isaiah 65:24

Risky!

It is a risky thing
to pray the Lord's Prayer
For to truly pray it
is to live it
in seeking justice

for the oppressed
in companionship with the lonely
in healing those who are hurt
That is the *life* of prayer
For it goes beyond
pious petitions
to a distant Deity
and instead incarnates
the life of the One
who for your sake
became poor
and suffered the cross
It is a risky thing
to pray
the
Lord's Prayer
But pray it
for My Holy Spirit
will teach you
how to pray
and then
how to *live*
that prayer[7]

Psalm 82:3   2 Corinthians 8:9

A *Different* Faith?

Beware of the cults
and new philosophies
of the day
And if you are struggling
with your faith
in Me
and feel you need
a *different* faith

know rather that
what you need is
a larger faith
a greater faith
a stronger faith
in Me
So search My Word
Pray
Relive your Baptism daily
Rejoice in the Eucharist
faithfully
And you will have
a larger faith
a greater faith
a stronger faith
in
Me

John 8:31-32   Colossians 2:8-9

"Why?" "Why *Not!*"

When I test you
remember
it's always in love
You are still My child!
And when
the going gets rough
don't say
"Why me Lord?"
but rather
"Why *not* me Lord?"
No masochism
No self pity
No martyr complex
Simply

"I accept Your test Lord
and I accept
Your promise
to be able
to bear it"
Why *not* me
Lord?

Matthew 26:39   2 Corinthians 4:17-18
Philippians 3:10   1 Peter 2:20-21

Complete Control

No matter
what happens to you
and your loved ones
remember
that you and they
are Mine
and I
I alone
am always
in control

1 Chronicles 29:11   Psalm 46   Psalm 62:2
Psalm 93   Isaiah 54:10

The Real Problem

The problem is not
that I don't know
or care about
what is going on
in your life
The real problem
is that you

don't really
trust in
and act
on
My promises

James 4:2b   *John 7:17*   *Deuteronomy 33:25, 27*
Isaiah 41:10   *1 Corinthians 10:13*

A Simple Question

I have
a simple question
for you
Are you willing
to be
a receiver
of
Me?

1 Samuel 3:18   *Job 1:21*   *Psalm 40:8*
Psalm 143:10   *John 7:17*   *Ephesians 6:6*

Prayer

Lord, direct me daily to the sources, the power supply, the Means of Your Grace by which I get to know You better: Your Holy Word and Sacraments. By the power of Your Holy Spirit help me become better acquainted with Your Son Jesus, that I may know Him and the power of His resurrection—and the way to eternal life. In the strong name of Jesus Christ. Amen.

THE CHRISTIAN ASKS—
Why am I so down, God?
GOD RESPONDS—

Sharing in Suffering

You and I know a woman
who is always cheerful
You can't understand that
when you see her suffer
and feel she has
reason to complain
Well you see
she is sharing
in My Son's sufferings
So though she does not
court her pain
she has
a kind of joy
which I give her
because she knows
we are in her trial
together
So by My power
it is always
a *corporate* victory!

Philippians 3:10-11   1 Peter 4:12-13

Silent Partner

As you drove your car
My angel protected you
As you did your work
My angel encouraged you
As you did your exercises
My angel empowered you
As you met discouragement
My angel ministered to you
As you went to sleep
My angel watched over you
And you thought
you were
alone?

Matthew 4:6, 11   Matthew 18:10

Solitude—Not Loneliness

Learn how to
accept the passing state
of loneliness
as a channel to
the wellspring of solitude
where you can savor
the freshness of
My Word and
the challenge of
knowing yourself better
Then you can
gear yourself up
for the new opportunities
I have planned
for you
But most of all

you have the chance
to get
better acquainted
with
Me[8]

Job 23:3   Jeremiah 29:13   Psalm 18:32
Psalm 30:11   Isaiah 34:16   Acts 17:11
Romans 15:4

"But What Did I Do Wrong?"

So your illness
your trial
your problem
has returned again
and you are wondering
what you
have been doing wrong?
That's not good thinking
I test the ones
I love
You are My child
I stretch
and pull
that you
may grow
Now I will not
test you
beyond your strength
But I promise
you will be
a better child
after
the experience

Hebrews 12   1 Corinthians 10:13

Some Identification!

You need courage?
Here
I will give it
to you
For I have
rolled up My sleeves
and entered humanity's affairs
in the person of
My Son
I have made
your experiences
My own
even to
the Cross
You need not
succumb to defeat
Jesus' victory
is already yours

Psalm 6:2   Hebrews 4:15-16

A Fellowship of Suffering

You are not alone
in a hostile world
You are part
of a fellowship
of suffering
throughout the world
You're not just
in the same boat together
Others in the church
worldwide
pray for you daily

You are not
alone
I hope
they are doing more
than just praying for you
Are you
for them?

1 Peter 5:9   *1 John 1:7*
Luke 10:36-37   *Galatians 6:2*

Prayer

When I am down, Lord, empower me by Your Holy Spirit to look *up* to the hills of Your strength. Make me know and assure me that I am never alone— but that You are always by my side. Bless me with the daily consciousness of Your holy angels who minister to me—as they did to Your Son, my Savior. In the strong name of Jesus Christ. Amen.

THE CHRISTIAN ASKS—
How can I relate better to others in my community, God?
GOD RESPONDS—

Waiting

They wait for you
today
The lonely widow
now forgotten
three weeks after
the funeral
The lonely boy
in the ghetto
with no father
The haggard mother
on welfare
The homesick
college student
miles from home
What I am
really saying is
I
am waiting
for
you

Matthew 25:40, 45

Slaves Nearby

Where are the slaves
near you
in your community?
Slaves
physically
emotionally
institutionally
politically?
And where are
the liberators?
Will you act
in Christ's name
saying
"I bring
Good News
to the poor
and release
for the captives"?
Will you
in His name
help usher in
"the acceptable
day
of the Lord"?

Isaiah 61:1-2   Luke 4:18-19   Matthew 25:40

No Ghettos

True spirituality is not
a state of mind
but an encounter
with flesh and blood persons
in the world

77

Your experience
Sunday morning
should not be
a ghetto
but wedded with
Monday's ministry
"Justice" is not
a sermon theme
but a dream actualized
in the giving
of your life
Christ not only spoke
He acted
in His community
and all the way
to Calvary

Psalm 82:3   John 10:10
1 Peter 2:24

Creeds or Deeds?

Do you
in your church
preach peace
when there is no peace?
Hope
where there is hopelessness
for so many
of the oppressed?
Freedom
while there is
oppression and enslavement?
Are you willing
to be broken
under the rod

with those suffering
injustice?
be hungry with the famished?
penniless with the impoverished?
Do you just
preach peace
or do you
pursue it?

Ezekiel 13:10   Psalm 34:14   Hebrews 4:12
1 John 3:18   Philippians 2:5-8

Pour Yourself Out!

Tell Me
one specific thing
you did
for someone else
today
Especially
the hungry
the homeless
the oppressed
the lonely
the self-centered
the "unlovable"
the unappreciative
the begrudging
the heartsick
Tell Me
one specific thing
you did
for someone else
today

Proverbs 21:13   Luke 6:35-36
Isaiah 58:10-12

That Carpenter's Son

Only when you are
involved
personally
in My church
and in the world
can you
help free people
see justice realized
raise the consciousness
of the bland
and lethargic
combat racism
and sexism
and fight dehumanization
at many levels
Only when you are
involved
personally
will it happen
as it did
with that
carpenter's son
from
Nazareth

Romans 8:32

Transformation

As you seek
to transform society
with My peace
and My love
you too

will be transformed
As you seek justice
for others
you yourself will become
more of a person of justice
As you seek peace
and pursue it
you will become
an individual of
gentleness and kindness
tenderness and love
For My Holy Spirit
will work in you
that which you
alone
are unable to do
and you will become
a light
a blessing
a "little Christ"
to others

Psalm 34:14   *Isaiah 58:10-12*   *Matthew 5:16*

No Private Connection

Your personal faith
in My Son
alone saves you
No one
can believe
for you
But your relationship
with Me
can never be
a solo trip

You are part
of My body
of believers
the Church
Christianity is societal
by nature
communal by definition
Live then
as a loving
vital
contributor
to My family

Habakkuk 2:4   Hebrews 10:25, 38

Holy Grace

Look back over
your pilgrimage
and see
the grace
that welled up
in the midst of your
lostness and pain
Look back
and see how
My Holy Spirit
rescued you
nurtured you
buoyed you
when you thought
all was lost
Look back
and remember
And now
look around you

to others
in their desolation
And be an instrument
of My
holy grace[9]

1 Chronicles 16:12   *Hebrews 11:1*
Revelation 2:5   *Matthew 20:28*

Pray and Act

Pray
and give of yourself
daily
to all My people
according to their needs
Pray for peace
and then work for it
Pray for justice
and then relieve
the oppressed
Pray for the poor
and then give them
such as you have
Pray for those
who do not believe in Me
and then relate to them
in love
Pray for the weary
Then help them
find rest
Pray for the lonely
Then comfort them
yourself
Pray for the sick
Then visit them

and help heal them
Pray always
But then
also
act

Matthew 25:36   *Acts 10:2*   *1 Thessalonians 5:17*
James 5:13-16   *1 John 3:18*

Self-Absorbed?

You may be
weak of faith
self-absorbed and
squeamish
about really reaching out
to the pain
of others
and it may take
the death of a loved one
to make you do it
But
keep your eyes open
to see the sorrow
in every life
(even the apparently unscathed)
Become sensitive to
the buried griefs
and hurtful memories
all around you
Reach out
and you *can*
alleviate pain
as did
My Son[9]

Galatians 6:2   *Matthew 8:16-17*

Use Those Muscles!

The church
doesn't need
your money
I certainly don't
Nevertheless
you should give
of what I
have given you
and not just
because there is
a need
but because
you need
to give
For you need
the spiritual exercise
So flex
those muscles
My church
will always
survive

Philippians 4:15-17   *Luke 6:30-38*
1 Peter 4:10

You!

Perhaps if you
you
do not personally
reach out to
the native Americans
the blacks
the Hispanics

the Asians
and many more
who are now
really quite near you
then
that person's potential
will never be realized
The urge to create
like a seed
in the soil
will wither and die
The ground will remain
unbroken
the promise unfulfilled
the idea
never expressed
the dream
dead
Perhaps if you
you
do not
personally
reach
out

Mark 10:43-44   Luke 10:36-37

Prayer

Move me out of the prison of my own little world, Lord, to the arena of sacrifice, self-giving, and service to Your suffering children. Teach me how to live not for myself but for others. Empower me—by Your Holy Spirit—not just to *speak*, but to *act*. In the strong name of Jesus Christ. Amen.

THE CHRISTIAN ASKS—
How should I view the world, God?
GOD RESPONDS—

Don't Get Squeezed

As you watch television
read newspapers and magazines
see a movie
listen to an ad
on the radio
Then consciously ask yourself
"Is that the meaning
and purpose of life?"
"Are those the values
My heavenly Father
wants me to pursue?"
Listen rather to My voice
in My Word
And don't let the world
around you
squeeze you
into its own mold
but let Me
remold your mind
from within
so that you may prove
in practice
that my plan for you
is good
and moves you
toward the goal
of true maturity

Romans 12:1-2

Think Globally

You may be proud
of your denomination
and I desire
your thankfulness
for the blessings
I have poured out
upon it
But your real
membership
is in My Body
of believers
all over
the world
Think globally then
of the thousands
starving daily
the hundreds dying daily
in one African nation alone
My children
Your brothers and sisters
That is your "denomination"
That is your family

Psalm 41:1   1 John 1:7

Open Trusting Kindness

You may need
bolts and locks
dogs and guns
to protect you
where you live
That grieves Me
But don't become
so cynical and callous

hostile and fearful
that you lose
the spirit
of open
trusting kindness
That's the ultimate answer
to the fear
and insecurity
of your age
It's risky
I know
But I sent My Son
into the same situation
Learn from Him
Open
trusting
kindness

Romans 12:10   *Ephesians 4:32*   *Colossians 3:12*

Toes Applecarts and Whirlwinds

I charge you
not to withdraw
from the world
Nor should you
identify with the world
and become
plaster saints
pagans with
a fringe on top
and the church
a comfort station
the tame captive
of the community

90

But rather
disturb the city
give it
an uneasy conscience
Not as a busybody
nor as a haughty self-righteous
finger-pointer
But draw your chair
up to the world
Speak from within it
fully involved
Challenge its
comfortable conscience
And though you
tread on toes
upset applecarts
start whirlwinds
and risk
censure criticism unpopularity
you will be doing
just what
My Son did
Go to it![10]

Acts 16:20   Luke 10:1, 17

Prayer

Give me the spectacles of Your Spirit, Lord, that I may see the world as it really is. Give me the grace to be *in* society while not succumbing *to* its values. Enable me to be Your agent—of truth and not compromise, of honest questions and not just dissent, of justice and mercy where there is prejudice and oppression. May I be a "little Christ," Lord. In the strong name of Jesus Christ. Amen.

THE CHRISTIAN ASKS—
How can I prepare
for the end, God?
GOD RESPONDS—

I Never Said That

I have never said
"you can't know
the joys of heaven
until you have
suffered the pangs
of hell"
Rather I say
now
is the day
of salvation
now
you are in
My care
My grace
My love
through your baptism
through your faith in
My Son
There is
no need
to fear
for I
am
near

Psalm 34:18   Psalm 85:9   2 Corinthians 6:2
Romans 6:4   Psalm 27:1

I Know

Your loved one
is gone
I know
And I know
in a way
you died too
For a little death
goes on each day
even though
the newspaper comes
the bills
must be paid
But the phone rings
less often
People "forget"
to drop in
Your loved one
is gone
I know
But I am with you
You may *feel* alone
at times
But you are never alone
Look to Me
and see[8]

2 Chronicles 15:2   Psalm 46   Hebrews 13:5b

"That's Great!"

His friends
at church
were baffled
when grandpa learned

he had pneumonia
and he said
"That's great!"
For he was
looking forward
to seeing Me
and knew his death
would not be
his own doing
But then he
caught his breath
and agonized over
the pain his loved ones
would experience
And He asked Me
to help them with that
So he had
two reactions
I think
"That's great!"

Philippians 1:21-25

You Just You

When I see you
face to face
I will not ask
why you were not
Mary
Peter
Dorcas
Paul
Luther
Bonhoeffer
Corrie ten Boom

C. S. Lewis
Mother Teresa
Rather
I will ask
why
were you not
you?

1 Corinthians 12:4   *Revelation 2:10*

This Day!

No matter what evil
you have done
in the past
you know I have fully
forgiven you
when you truly
repented
Now I have
permitted you
to see
this day
Savor it
Rejoice in it
Use it wisely
It will never
come again
So enjoy
My gift
of living
one more day!
And praise Me
the Giver

Luke 12:20   Joshua 24:15   Psalm 130:4
Psalm 146:2   Psalm 118:24

The Signs

You asked
for a sign
from Me?
But do you
not see
nation fighting nation
brother against brother
famines earthquakes
persecution
false prophets?
You asked
for a sign
from Me?
Your age has
the signs
and *your* age
is a sign also
Just look
in a mirror
But also remember
though now you see
through a glass darkly
soon you will see Me
face to face
My Beloved!

Matthew 24   Psalm 71:9
Ecclesiastes 12:1   Isaiah 46:4

Ascendant Journey

A boy feared
the dark
at the top

of the stairs
But you can have
that dread
of the unknown dispelled
as you make
your ascendant journey
towards Me
For you know
My love for you
I have cared
and will care
for you
through the tomb
and beyond
For I have promised
I will never
leave you
nor
forsake you

Matthew 10:28   *John 14:1-3, 27*
Psalm 37:28   *Hebrews 13:5*

The Best = The Best

At times
it may be hard
to believe that
the best of your life
is the rest of your life
But it can be
if you
thank Me
for the past
Live today
for itself

grateful
for My blessings
And know that
the best
is yet
to come
Even I can
hardly
wait!

Philippians 1:23   *Colossians 4:2*
John 14:2-3

Welcome Home!

You and others
were always impressed
by that famous Christian
who just died
Well
up here
she's not "famous"
for that concept
doesn't exist up here
But is she cherished?
Fulfilled?
Joyous?
Exuberant in
reunion with
her fellow saints?
Yes!
Now
we are waiting
for
you!

John 11:25   *1 Thessalonians 4:16-17*
Isaiah 57:2   *Revelation 21:1-4*

I'll Be Seeing You

I am coming again
so watch and pray
Always be ready
Stand on tiptoe
like a bride
awaiting the bridegroom
It will be
a joyous reunion
So watch and pray
Don't be fearful
rather always
look for Me
with
joyous hope

Luke 21:9, 34-36   1 Thessalonians 4:13-18

A Reason to Die

What would you
really die for?
Think about it
What would you
really *die* for?
My Son died
even for those
who
ultimately
deny and reject
Him
Now that's love
What would you
really
die for?

John 15:13

Prayer

Give me the long-range view, O Lord, the eternal perspective of preparing for the life to come in Your presence, and yet living each day here and now for itself. Make me mindful of past blessings and content with Your plan for my life today. As I watch and pray daily for Your return, may I never live in fear or anxiety, but always in joyful anticipation of the grandest family reunion of them all. In the strong name of Jesus Christ. Amen.

THE CHRISTIAN SAYS—
Tell me once again, God!
GOD RESPONDS—

Just Go!

Now that you
have heard My words
of care and affection
for you again
can you keep
the Good News
to yourself?
Tell your brothers
and sisters about Me
and how you've come
to think of Me
Dare to share
the Message
Don't look for
or expect "results"
Just
go
and
tell
And I promise
My Spirit
will
attend you

Matthew 10:7, 27   Mark 16:15   Luke 9:2, 60
Acts 4:20   1 Timothy 3:13   2 Timothy 4:2

Loosen Up!

Are you lighthearted
or humorless?
Are you unbending
or easygoing?
Perfectionist
or admittedly fallible?
Do you know the luxury
of being wrong?
admitting a mistake?
Now I'm not just
"in the business
of forgiveness"
But when you truly repent
I joyously absolve you
So loosen up!
You are in the orbit
of My grace
and My love

1 John 1:8-9   John 8:32   Romans 8:2, 21
2 Corinthians 3:17

Look More Closely

If you don't think
someone near you
needs you
just look
a
little harder
My Son came
not to be
ministered unto
but to minister

His sheep
and lambs
are nearer to you
than
you
think

Matthew 20:28   *John 21:16*
Matthew 5:42

Who Are Your Friends?

So you see
I am the God
of the oppressed
the God of the
underdog
I am
the God of the
impoverished
Haven't you
really read
the Gospels?
Look again
at whom
My Son
consorted with
Now who are *your* friends?
I do not despise
the rich
They are My friends
too
But how many
of the *really* poor
are your *personal*
friends?

And what
are you doing
to
help
them?
Now?
Today?

Matthew 10:42   Matthew 11:19
John 13:5

The Most Necessary Trip

You cannot remove
your guilt
by forgetting it
projecting it
ignoring it
burying it
But take a trip
to Calvary
See it forgiven
erased
forgotten
forever
That's how I
handle guilt

Psalm 51:1   Acts 3:19
Isaiah 43:25

Excitement

Would you like
the excitement
the exhilaration

the exuberance
of helping people
with their potential
and then seeing
the excitement
the exhilaration
the exuberance
of their blossoming
under your
encouraging care?
They are there!

Galatians 6:2, 10   Psalm 100:2
Acts 21:17

Give or Take?

Do you just
take what
you want?
Or do you
give
what
I think
is
needed?

Luke 6:30-38

"What Time Is It?"

Watch the
second hand
of a clock
Each minute
once gone

can never
be retrieved
or lived again
What are you
living for
right now?

Matthew 19:21   *Matthew 24:42*
Luke 12:15-21

Prayer

I need to hear some things over and over again from You, Lord. Especially that You still love me although I've so often failed You. And as I have listened to Your mighty promises in Your Word, I am assured again that You do! Thank You, Lord! Forgive me for my doubting, my failure, my self-centeredness, Lord! Now, move me! Empower me with Your Holy Spirit! Send me out, Lord! To do *Your* will, not mine. In the strong name of Jesus Christ. Amen.

THE CHRISTIAN ASKS—
What else do I need to hear from You, God?
GOD RESPONDS—

A Warning—A Promise

If you really
love Me
because you think
I am
a fairly indulgent parent
Remember that
in my love
for you
I have some plans
in mind
They will not be
more than you
can handle
But they may
surprise you
So
don't take My grace
lightly
I am with you
But I
am not mocked
My warning is
"You can't fool Me"
My Good News is
"You don't have to"

Galatians 6:7   Jeremiah 29:11

Real Life

Real life means
putting up with
real people
real sins and
real forgiveness
You will face
misunderstanding
friction
hostility
tragedy
But I call you
to live this day
this hour
this moment
responsibly and
constructively
grounded in My Word
heartened by My promises
filled with My peace

Colossians 3:12-17

Do You Really?

Do you really
love Me?
(You say
you do)
Do you really
love Me?
(You say
you do)
Do you really
love Me?

(You say
you do)
Then why
aren't you
doing
what
I
want
you
to
do?

John 21:15-17   *Matthew 22:37-40*

The Mystery and the Hope

In reaching out
you are reached
In giving
you receive
In changing
you are changed
In loving
you are loved
In saving
you are saved
In serving
you are fulfilled
Christ in you
The mystery
and
the hope
of
the
world

Matthew 7:7-8   *Colossians 1:27*

Prayer

How wonderful to get to know You better, Lord! Now I am going back to Your Word and again rediscover and then act on Your promises and challenges to me. O Blessed Lord, make me a daily receiver of Your Holy Spirit that I may do Your will in my own household and also out in the world—the world Your Son suffered and died for. Change me, Lord! Move me, Lord! Use me, Lord! I'm ready now, Lord! In the strong name of Jesus Christ! Amen!

Let us bless the Lord! Thanks be to God!

Acknowledgements

The following were instrumental in providing inspiration for some of the meditations in this volume.
1. Walter R. Wietzke, *Believers Incorporated: The Message of Ephesians for Evangelical Outreach* (Minneapolis: Augsburg 1977), p. 21.
2. Lee C. Moorhead, "The Bland Leading the Bland," (*The Pulpit*, April 1958)
3. Peter A. Bertocci, "What Makes a Christian Home?" (*The Christian Century*, May 6, 1959).
4. David J. Maitland, "Free to Love" (*The Pulpit*, June 1959), p. 17.
5. T. S. Eliot, *The Cocktail Party* (New York: Harcourt Brace, 1964).
6. Andrew M. Greeley, *The Cardinal Sins* (New York: Warner Books, 1981), pp. 349—350.
7. Theodore P. Jennings Jr., "Prayer: The Call for God" (*The Christian Century*, April 15, 1981), p. 413.
8. Elisabeth Elliot, "The Ones Who Are Left" (*Christianity Today*, Feb. 27, 1976), p. 7.
9. Frederick Buechner, *The Sacred Journey* (San Francisco: Harper and Row, 1982), pp. 56, 57.
10. J. A. Davidson, "Keeping the World's Conscience Uneasy" (*The Pulpit*, May 1959), p. 18.
Acknowledgment is also given for ideas from unpublished manuscripts or comments made by: Robert E. Lee, Atlanta, Ga.; John Nierman, Wichita, Kans.; Martin Luther King Jr.; Robert K. Menzel, Tacoma, Wash.; Martin Luther; Sharon Streater, Berkeley, Calif.; and especially Corinne Deffner and David Owren, Moraga and Orinda, Calif.